16/11/20

Please return/renew this item by the
last date shown to avoid a charge.
Books may also be renewed by phone
and Internet. May not be renewed if
required by another reader.

www.libraries.barnet.gov.uk

BARNET
LONDON BOROUGH

A World of Food

INDIA

Anita Ganeri

First published in paperback in 2015

First published in 2010 by Franklin Watts

Franklin Watts
338 Euston Road
London NW1 3BH

Franklin Watts Australia
Level 17/207 Kent Street, Sydney, NSW 2000

Produced by Arcturus Publishing Limited,
26/27 Bickels Yard, 151–153 Bermondsey Street, London SE1 3HA

Series concept: Alex Woolf
Editor: Alex Woolf
Designer: Jane Hawkins
Map illustrator: Stefan Chabluk
Picture researcher: Alex Woolf

Picture Credits
Bridgeman Art Library: 7 (British Library, London), 9 (The Stapleton Collection).
Corbis: 4 (Hans Georg Roth), 6 (Roger Wood), cover and 8 (Bennett Dean/Eye Ubiquitous), 10 (Frédéric Soltan), 11 (David Jay Zimmerman), 12 (Adam Woolfitt), 15 (Lindsay Hebberd), 16 (Jeremy Horner), 17 (John and Lisa Merrill), 18 (Dave Bartruff), 20 (Bob Krist), 23 (Amit Bhargava), 27 (Michael Boys), 28 (Gail Mooney).
Getty Images: 22 (Prakash Singh/AFP), 24 (Narinder Nanu/AFP).
Shutterstock: 3 *left* (Agb), 3 *right* (Joe Gough), 4 *decorative* (Sasha Davas), 8 *decorative* (Sasha Davas), 13 *basmati rice* (Harm Kruyshaar), 13 *lentils* (Marta Tobolova), 13 *cinnamon, cloves, ginger* (Elena Schweitzer), 13 *kitchri* (Sasha Davas), 14 (Kharidehal Abhirama Ashwin), 19 *potatoes* (Denis Dryashkin), 19 *tomatoes* (Valentin Mosichev), 19 *garam masala, coriander, turmeric* (elena moiseeva), 19 *cauliflower* (Denis Pepin), 19 *aloo gobi* (Monkey Business Images), 20 *decorative* (Sasha Davas), 21 *milk* (Jozsef Szasz-Fabian), 21 *coconut flakes* (Maja Schon), 21 *sugar* (Danny Smythe), 21 *almonds, pistachios* (Elena Schweitzer), 21 *butter* (Shebeko), 21 *coconut barfi* (Paul Cowan), 25 (Chin Kit Sen), 26 *decorative* (Sasha Davas), 26 *left* (Sid B Viswakumar), 26 *right* (Monkey Business Images), 29 (NZG), 31 *bottom centre* (Joe Gough), *bottom right* (Sasha Davas).

A CIP catalogue record for this book is available from the British Library.

Dewey Decimal Classification Number: 394.1'2'0954

ISBN 978 1 4451 4491 7

Printed in China

Franklin Watts is a division of Hachette Children's Books, an Hachette UK company.
www.hachette.co.uk

SL001037UK
Supplier 29, Date 0315, Print run 4039

Contents

India is a vast country, the largest in South Asia and the seventh biggest in the world. It is home to more than a billion people, making it the world's second most populated country.

▲ An Indian family eat a traditional meal in a restaurant.

India is also an ancient land, with a history stretching back more than 5,000 years. Because of its huge size, population and long history, India is a land of immense variety. Nowhere is this more obvious than in the enormous range of Indian food.

Land and landscape

India is shaped roughly like a diamond, and covers an area of some 3,288,000 square kilometres, more than a third of the size of the United States. The landscape is very varied, ranging from snow-capped mountains to scorching deserts and tropical rainforests. There are three main geographical regions. The first is the Himalayas, the world's highest mountain range, which marks India's northern boundary. The second is the flat, fertile Indo-Gangetic Plain, crossed by the River Ganges on its way from the Himalayas to the Bay of Bengal. The third region is the Deccan Plateau, a large area of raised land to the south of the plain.

Food and influence

Food plays an vital part in Indian cultural life and religion. Like the country itself, food varies greatly from place to place and is influenced by each region's particular terrain, climate and crops. Today, Indian food has also become popular around the world, as Indians have moved away from India and settled in other countries.

► This map shows the vast country of India with its many different regions.

SOME COMMON INDIAN FOODS

Word	Pronunciation	Meaning
aloo	aa-loo	potato
chaaval	chaa-wul	rice
dahi	da-hee	yogurt
dhal	daal	a thick stew made from pulses, onions and spices
gobi	go-bee	cauliflower
mirch	meerch	chilli
roti	ro-tee	bread

History of Indian Food

Over thousands of years, India has attracted many traders and explorers, as well as invading peoples who went on to rule the country. Each brought their own culture and religion with them and left their particular mark on Indian food. Many of the dishes eaten in India today date from ancient times.

Ancient farmers

The Indus Valley civilization flourished along the banks of the River Indus in about 2500 BCE. Using water from the river for irrigation, people were able to grow crops, such as wheat, barley, melons and dates, on the fertile plains.

▼ The ruins of the granaries (grain stores) in the Indus Valley city of Harappa.

In about 1500 BCE, people known as Aryans from Central Asia began to invade the Indus Valley. Their period of dominance, which lasted until around 500 BCE, was called the Vedic period, after the Vedas, the Aryans' sacred texts. They grew crops and hunted forest animals for meat. Many hymns in praise of food can be found in the Vedas, as well as hymns of thanks for a good harvest.

Mogul cuisine

During the 16th century, much of India was conquered by the Moguls, a group of Muslims who invaded from the north-west. The Mogul empire was famed for its beautiful buildings, glittering courts and sumptuous feasts. At a banquet held by the great emperor, Akbar, it is said that some 500 dishes were served. Some of India's most delicious dishes, including pilafs and biryanis, date from this time.

AYURVEDIC FOOD

Ayurveda is the ancient Indian system of medicine. Different foods are classified as heavy, light, warm or cool, according to their effects on the body and mind. Good health can be achieved by eating the correct foods at the correct times. For example, 'warm' foods are good for fuelling the body in winter; 'cool' foods are best eaten in the summer heat.

▶ A painting of a Mogul emperor and his courtiers enjoying a lavish feast.

Europeans and Spices

In 1498 the Portuguese navigator and merchant, Vasco da Gama, landed at Calicut on the west coast of India, becoming the first European to reach India by sea. Over the next 450 years, many more European traders and settlers followed, including the French and British. Their influence on Indian culture and food can still be seen.

The spice trade

The reason for da Gama's voyage was to find a new route to the East Indies (an old name for India and South-East Asia), which was the source of the precious spices arriving in Europe. India was crucial to the spice trade.

▶ A market in India selling spices used to flavour Indian food.

INDIAN SPICES

Spices are an essential part of Indian cooking and are used to give a delicious flavour to even very simple dishes. The most important and frequently used spices are cumin, coriander, asafoetida, turmeric, fenugreek, ginger, mustard seed, cardamom and chillies. Chillies originally grew in South America and were introduced to India by the Portuguese.

Cloves and nutmegs from the East Indies were brought to southern India, where black pepper and cinnamon were added to the cargo to be shipped to Europe. From their base on the west coast, the Portuguese were able to control this extremely valuable trade.

The British Raj

The British arrived in India as traders in the 17th century and gradually strengthened their position and power. In 1858, the British parliament took control of the country. Thousands of people from Britain made the long journey to live and work in India. Many tried to live as they had at home, cooking and eating the same food. Other dishes were influenced by Indian recipes. Some of these, such as kedgeree (a dish of rice, fish, egg and curry powder) and chutney (fruit pickle) are still eaten today.

◀ This 19th-century British family in India are eating a similar breakfast to the one they would have eaten at home.

Because it is such a vast country, India's climate varies considerably. It is generally a hot country, with the highest temperatures in the west and south. In the mountainous far north, however, snow falls in winter and temperatures can plunge to below -20°C.

Winter and summer

The Indian year is divided into four seasons. Winter lasts from January to March. Temperatures range from 15°C in the north-west to 25°C in the south-east. Summer lasts from March to June. April and May are the hottest months, with average temperatures of 30–40°C in the interior.

Monsoon

The monsoon (rainy) season lasts from June to September. South-westerly winds bring torrential rain that sweeps across the country, bringing vital water for farmers' crops. If the rains are particularly heavy, fields and crops may be swept away. If the rains fail, crops die and people face hunger and drought. The post-monsoon

◀ Monsoon rains fall on a market in Kolkata, India.

season lasts from October to December, bringing drier, less humid weather.

Soil and crops

India has a wide range of soils, depending on location and climate. Alluvial and black soils are the best for crops. Alluvial soils are deposited by rivers flowing from the Himalayas and are particularly good for growing wheat, rice, pulses and sugar cane. Black soils are named after their colour but are also known as cotton soils. They are good for growing cotton, cereals, oil seeds and vegetables.

▼ Women working in paddy (rice) fields in West Bengal, India.

STORM DANGER

With its fertile soil and plentiful water supply, the low-lying land around the Bay of Bengal in the west of India is ideal for growing rice. But the region is regularly hit by violent tropical storms, called cyclones, especially in September or October. These cause terrible floods that devastate the countryside, bringing disaster to farmers.

Farming and Crops

Around 60 per cent of Indians work as farmers or depend on agriculture for their living. Most farms are fairly small areas of land that provide crops for families to eat and sell. Children often help their parents in the fields after school.

Farming methods

Many Indian farmers are poor and cannot afford to buy modern farming equipment. Many still rely on traditional bullock ploughs to work their land rather than expensive tractors.

Main crops

The main crops grown in India are rice, wheat and pulses such as lentils and chickpeas. These are staple ingredients in the Indian diet. Cotton, jute, sugar cane and tea are grown largely for export – India is the world's leading producer of tea.

India is the world's second largest grower of rice. In many Indian households, it is eaten with almost every meal. More rice is eaten in the south, where it is widely grown. The most popular variety of rice is basmati, which grows in the foothills of the Himalayas. There are hundreds of different rice dishes. One of the most popular is called *kitchri*.

▶ A farmer uses a traditional bullock plough to prepare his fields for planting crops.

RECIPE: kitchri

Equipment
- chopping board • knife • bowl • measuring jug
- large saucepan • wooden spoon • fork • clean tea towel

Ingredients (serves 6)
- 60g yellow or green lentils
- 3 tablespoons vegetable oil • 1 teaspoon cumin seeds
- 6 cloves • $\frac{1}{2}$ cinnamon stick • 2 onions (finely chopped)
- 2 cloves garlic (finely chopped)
- 2cm piece of ginger (finely chopped)
- 300g basmati rice (washed)
- 1 teaspoon garam masala
- 3 tablespoons lemon juice
- salt and ground black pepper

Ask a grown-up to help you with the chopping and hot oil.

1 Put the lentils in a bowl with 500ml of water. Leave to soak for 2 hours.

2 Heat the oil in saucepan and gently fry the cumin seeds, cloves and cinnamon for a few seconds.

3 Turn up the heat slightly and add the onion, garlic and ginger. Cook until they soften and begin to go brown.

4 Add the rice and lentils. Toss to coat thoroughly in oil.

5 Add garam masala, lemon juice and 750ml of boiling water. Bring to the boil, then cover and simmer for 15 minutes.

6 Remove the pan from the heat and gently fluff up the mixture with a fork.

7 Cover the pan with a clean tea towel and leave for 10 minutes.

8 Fluff up again and season with salt and pepper. Serve with yogurt.

Culture and Etiquette

Most Indians like to eat three meals a day – breakfast, lunch and dinner. Breakfast may be toast, eggs and fruit, or, more traditionally, reheated bread, rice and vegetables from the day before. Lunch and dinner are usually full meals.

An Indian meal

An Indian meal varies greatly from region to region. Food is traditionally served on a thali (a large, metal plate), with helpings of different dishes served in small metal bowls. In south India, a banana leaf is sometimes used instead of a thali. The dishes may include several vegetable or meat dishes, accompanied by dhal, raita or yogurt, poppadoms, pickles and rice or bread. Water is the most common drink with food.

Although most Indians still cook and eat food at home, restaurants are also popular. In big cities these include Westernized fast-food restaurants serving pizzas and burgers. To suit Indian tastes, however, pizzas may come with extra chilli, and burgers are made with chicken rather than beef (see page 17).

◄ A typical thali from northern India.

Eating Indian style

Traditionally, Indians do not use cutlery to eat but use the fingers of their right hands. (Their left hands are considered unclean.) They tear off a piece of bread to scoop up food, or mix the food with rice, then scoop it up. It is said that food tastes better this way, and you do not eat food that is too hot. Today, many Indians also use knives and forks.

▼ A woman makes chapattis (bread) in her traditional kitchen.

INDIAN BREAD

There are many different types of Indian bread. Most are unleavened (not made to rise with yeast). Bread is particularly popular in north India where the land and climate are mostly unsuitable for growing rice.

- chapatti: a round flatbread, cooked on a *tava* (metal hot plate)
- nan: a puffy bread, made with yeast and cooked in a tandoor (clay oven)
- paratha: like a chapatti but richer; may be plain or stuffed with vegetables
- *phulka*: a type of chapatti that is made to puff up
- puri: small, puffy bread that is deep-fried in hot oil
- kulcha: a leavened bread traditionally cooked in a wood-fired oven

Food and Religion

Food is very closely associated with religion in India, and religious beliefs often dictate which foods people can and cannot eat. More than 80 per cent of Indians are Hindus. They follow the ancient religion of Hinduism that began in India more than 5,000 years ago.

▲ A market stall selling fruit and vegetables, very important ingredients in Indian cooking.

Vegetarianism

The vast majority of Hindus are vegetarians. They believe it is important to respect all living things, which means not harming or killing them. Some Hindus eat chicken and fish, especially if they live along the coast. Others are such strict vegetarians that they will not even use onions or garlic to flavour food because these two ingredients are associated with cooking meat.

▲ A sacred cow and its calf being fed outside a house in Jaisalmer, India.

Even if some Hindus eat chicken and fish, they do not eat beef. They believe that cows are sacred animals because they produce milk, a very precious source of nourishment. Foods made from cow's milk, such as yogurt, cheese and ghee (clarified butter), feature regularly in the Indian diet. In India, cows can often be seen wandering the streets, feeding on vegetable scraps.

Sacred food

Food plays an important part in Hindu worship. Many Hindus go to a *mandir* (temple) to worship, believing that the *mandir* is God's home on Earth. Each *mandir* is dedicated to a Hindu deity, and a *murti* (sacred image) of the deity stands in the main shrine. Through the *murti*, God is believed to accept the worshipper's love and devotion.

Worshippers take a donation of fruit, rice, flowers or money to offer to the deity. The food is used by the priest to prepare meals to offer to the deity. It then becomes *prasad* (sacred food). Part of it is handed back to worshippers as they leave the *mandir*.

Other Religions

Apart from Hindus, millions of Muslims, Sikhs, Buddhists and Jains also live in India. Their religions have their own rules and traditions associated with food.

Muslim food

About 11 per cent of Indians are Muslims, who follow the religion of Islam. The Quran, the sacred book of Islam, sets out many rules about food and drink. Food that Muslims are allowed to eat is called halal; forbidden food is haram. Muslims eat meat, as long as the meat is halal and the animal is killed in a particular way. Pork, however, is always haram, and most meat dishes are made with lamb, mutton or chicken.

Sikh and Jain food

Like Hindus, Sikhs and Jains are vegetarians because they do not believe in killing living things to eat. Jains are particularly strict and go to great lengths to prevent animals from being harmed as they prepare their food. For example, some Jains do not eat vegetables such as potatoes and onions, that grow underground, because insects and small animals may be harmed when the plants are pulled up.

▶ After worship in the gurdwara, Sikhs share a meal of bread and vegetable dishes.

RECIPE: aloo gobi

This is a popular vegetable dish in India.

Equipment
- chopping board • knife • deep frying pan or wok
- wooden spoon • measuring jug

Ingredients (serves 4)
- 3 tablespoons vegetable oil
- 1/2 teaspoon black mustard seeds
- 200g potatoes (peeled and cut into cubes)
- 1/4 teaspoon ground turmeric
- 1 teaspoon ground coriander
- 1 teaspoon ground cumin
- 1 1/2 teaspoons garam masala
- 4 large, ripe tomatoes, chopped
- 1 large cauliflower, cut into florets
- 2cm piece fresh ginger (peeled and finely chopped)

Ask a grown-up to help you with the chopping and hot oil.

1 Heat oil in frying pan and add mustard seeds. Wait for seeds to pop.

2 Add potatoes. Fry until lightly browned.

3 Add remaining spices and fry for a few seconds.

4 Add the chopped tomato and stir well.

5 Add the cauliflower and stir well.

6 Stir in ginger and 125ml water. Turn up the heat and bring to the boil.

7 Reduce heat, cover pan and simmer for 15 minutes.

8 Season with salt and pepper. Serve with chapattis and yogurt.

Hindu Festivals

There are thousands of festivals throughout the year in India. Some Hindu festivals celebrate events in the lives of the deities; others are linked to the changing seasons, harvest time or family events. Hindu festivals are lively, joyful times in which food plays an important part.

Festival food

Diwali is one of the most important festivals for Hindus. It is celebrated in October or November. Hindus remember the story of the god, Rama, and his wife, Sita, and their triumphant return from exile. They light lamps, called *divas*, to help guide the couple home.

In India, Diwali celebrations can last up to five days. People visit the *mandir*, exchange gifts and cards, visit friends and relatives, and eat special food. Diwali is especially associated with Indian sweets. They are given as gifts when people go visiting, and as offerings in the *mandir*.

◄ A young girl sells *diva* lamps at Diwali. Diwali is also known as the 'festival of lights'.

Indian sweets

During the run-up to Diwali, thousands of kilograms of sweets are made. Indian sweets are made from milk, curd cheese, coconut, nuts and sugar. Those made for festivals like Diwali may be beautifully decorated with wafer-thin layers of real silver leaf, nuts, dried fruits and saffron.

RECIPE: coconut barfi

Equipment
- saucepan • wooden spoon • baking tray
- greaseproof paper

Ingredients
- 250ml full-fat milk • 500g caster sugar
- 1 tablespoon butter
- 100g dessicated coconut
- 50g almonds and pistachio nuts (finely chopped) • 500g powdered milk

Ask a grown-up to help you with the chopping.

1 Put the milk in a saucepan and heat gently. Add the sugar and bring to the boil, stirring all the time.

2 Reduce to a simmer and add the butter. Stir until it melts.

3 Add dessicated coconut and chopped nuts.

4 Take pan off heat. Gradually add powdered milk.

5 Line baking tray with greaseproof paper. Pour mixture in and spread out evenly.

6 Leave the mixture in the fridge to cool. This will take several hours.

7 Cut the *barfi* into diamond shapes. Serve cold.

Other Festivals

Food plays a key part in festivals celebrated by the followers of other Indian religions, such as Muslims, Sikhs and Jains. Fasting (going without food) is also very important.

Muslim festivals

The Muslim festival of Id ul-Fitr marks the end of Ramadan, the month of fasting. During Ramadan, most Muslims fast from daybreak to sunset every day. They believe that by fasting, they learn self-discipline and not to be selfish or greedy. At sunset they break their fast with a simple meal of dates and water, followed by an evening meal.

On the morning of Id ul-Fitr, Muslims visit the mosque to pray. Afterwards, there are Id parties, with new clothes, gifts and delicious Id feasts. The type of food served varies from place to place, but in India, a sweet pudding, made with rice or fine pasta, nuts and raisins, is very popular.

▶ Muslims in India celebrate the festival of Id ul-Fitr with a meal.

▼ A man prepares the traditional sweet, jalebi, for the Sikh festival of Hola Mohalla.

Sikh festivals

Sikh festivals remember key times in the lives of the gurus (Sikh religious teachers) and other great events in Sikh history. Many festivals are celebrated with worship in the gurdwara (temple), with prayer, hymns and a reading of the Guru Granth Sahib, the Sikhs' holy book. At the end, a sweet mixture called *karah parshad* is shared out. *Karah parshad* is made from sugar, butter and semolina, cooked until the mixture goes thick. For Sikhs, the act of sharing *karah parshad* is a way of showing that everyone is equal.

FESTIVAL FASTING

During the festival of Paryushan, some strict Jains fast for eight days, living only on boiled water. Others may fast on a few of the days. Some Jains do not fast at all but have even more restrictions on the food that they can eat. For example, they do not eat green vegetables or herbs to avoid harming any insects that live on the plants' leaves.

Because India is such a huge country, food varies enormously from region to region. Climate, soil and local produce all influence what people cook and eat. As well as dishes found throughout the country, each region has its own speciality dishes and cooking styles.

▲ An Indian baker making traditional kulcha breads, which he bakes in his tandoor oven.

Tandoori cooking

Tandoori cooking was introduced to north-west India by the Moguls (see page 7). It involves cooking food in a clay oven, called a tandoor, over charcoal. Meat, such as chicken or lamb, is marinated in yogurt and spices before it is cooked. This style of cooking gives the meat a delicious, smoky flavour and makes it tender and succulent. Nan and other breads are baked by being pressed against the wall of the tandoor.

Desert staples

The state of Rajasthan in north-west India is largely covered in dry desert. Few crops can grow in the harsh climate so people have become expert at drying and preserving vegetables. Pulses, such as lentils and chickpeas, also play a large part in the diet. One of the region's best-known dishes is *dal-baati-churma*, a dhal made with five types of lentils. Lots of oil and butter are used in cooking because water is in short supply.

Food from the east

The state of West Bengal in north-east India is famous for its sweets, particularly *rasgullas* and *sandesh*. *Rasgullas* are small balls of curd cheese and sugar that are cooked in sugar syrup until they are spongy. *Sandesh* is also made from curd cheese and sugar, flavoured with ingredients such as coconut, nuts and rose water, and shaped in moulds.

▼ A selection of mouth-watering sweets on sale at a roadside stall.

Both the south and west of India have distinctive dishes and cooking styles. These are not only influenced by local crops and conditions, but by the traders, invaders and settlers who have left their mark on these regions.

Southern food

Together with pulses and vegetables, rice is the main ingredient in much of the food of south India. Popular dishes include idlis and dosas, which are often eaten for breakfast. Idlis are small, steamed rice cakes, usually eaten with coconut chutney. Dosas are large, spongy rice pancakes, often filled with spicy potatoes and served with *sambhar* (south Indian dhal).

▲ A typical breakfast from south India, consisting of idlis, served with chutney and a sauce.

▶ A dish of dosas with spicy potatoes.

Hundreds of years ago, the city of Hyderabad in the state of Andhra Pradesh was ruled by Muslim kings. Many of its dishes were influenced by Muslim cuisine. The most famous is biryani, a rich dish made from rice and meat, which is often cooked at festival times.

Food from the West

The food of Goa on the west coast of India is influenced by the cooking of the Portuguese who lived in the area for hundreds of years. The region's most famous dish is vindaloo, which is based on a Portuguese meat stew, made with garlic and wine. It is extremely hot and fiery and is usually made with pork. The meat is marinated in spices overnight, then cooked very slowly with onions.

STREET FOOD

On street corners in every Indian city, there are stalls selling food. This ranges from simple bags of puffed rice to fried pakoras, or plates of rice and dhal. Each region has its speciality snacks. Mumbai, in western India, is famous for its *vada-pao*. This is a deep-fried spicy lentil fritter (vada), sandwiched between two pieces of bread (*pao*).

▼ A street stall in Mumbai, India, selling a selection of snacks.

Many Indians have settled in other parts of the world, taking their food and cooking techniques with them. Today, Indian food has become hugely popular in countries such as Britain and the United States, and there are thousands of Indian restaurants.

▲ A row of Indian restaurants in New York City, USA. Indian food has become very popular in many countries around the world.

Indian origins?

Most 'Indian' restaurants do not serve the vegetarian food eaten by the majority of Indians. They have adapted their dishes to suit Western tastes. Many of these restaurants are run by people from Bangladesh, to the east of India, and Kashmir, to the north. Diners who enjoy 'Indian' food often get a shock when they actually visit India and taste the food!

Popular dishes

Two of the most popular dishes served in Indian restaurants are chicken tikka masala and baltis. In fact, chicken tikka masala has become the most popular dish served in any type of British restaurant. To make the dish, chunks of chicken are marinated in spices and yogurt, then cooked in a tandoor. The chicken is served in a spicy cream and tomato sauce and eaten with rice or nan bread.

▲ Chicken tikka masala served with rice and garnished with coriander leaves.

A balti is a spicy dish, made with meat or vegetables. It takes its name from the two-handled metal bowl in which it is cooked and served. In several Indian languages, *balti* means 'bucket'. The dish is normally served with naan bread, which is used to scoop up the food. It is thought that balti cooking originally came from north-west India. It first appeared in the West in the 1960s when people from that region settled in England.

WHAT IS CURRY?

The word *curry* is used in the West to describe any spicy Indian dish. But there is no such dish as a curry in authentic Indian cooking. It is thought that the word comes from south India, from the Tamil word *kari*, which means a dish served in a sauce or gravy.

Glossary

biryani A dish that is made with rice and meat or fish.

civilization A human society that is highly advanced and organized.

clarified butter Butter that has been heated to make it clear.

climate The type of weather a place has over a long period of time.

deity A god or a goddess.

dessicated Dried or powdered. Dessicated coconut is often an ingredient in Indian sweets.

etiquette A set of customs or rules about how to behave.

export Sell goods to another country.

fertile Describes land where crops grow well.

garam masala A mixture of spices used in Indian cooking.

gurdwara A place of worship for Sikhs.

humid Describes hot, sticky conditions, when the air is filled with moisture.

irrigation Supplying land with water so that crops can grow.

jute A plant grown for its fibres, which are used to make rope and sacks.

kitchri A dish made with rice, pulses and spices.

mandir A place of worship for Hindus.

marinated When meat or fish is soaked in a sauce before cooking.

mosque A place of worship for Muslims.

murti A sacred image of a deity that stands in a Hindu *mandir*.

navigator In olden times, another name for an experienced sailor.

pakora A piece of vegetable or meat, coated in seasoned batter and deep-fried.

phulka A type of puffed-up chapatti.

pilaf A rich dish made from rice and meat, flavoured with spices.

plateau A large area of raised, mostly flat land.

poppadom A flat, round wafer eaten at the end of meals.

pulses Edible seeds, such as split peas, beans and lentils.

Quran The sacred book of Islam.

Raj The period of British rule in India that lasted from 1858 until 1947.

staple A food that forms the basis of the diet of the people of a particular country or region.

tava A metal hot plate, used for cooking chapattis.

thali A large, round metal plate on which meals are served.

vegetarian Someone who does not eat meat.

Further Information

Books

Cooking Around the World: Cooking the Indian Way by Vijay Madavan (Lerner Books, 2009)

Food and Celebrations: India by Sylvia Goulding (Wayland, 2008)

Superchef: The Cooking of India by Matthew Locricchio (Marshall Cavendish Children's Books, 2004)

A Taste of Culture: Foods of India by Barbara Sheen (Kidhaven Press, 2006)

World of Recipes: India by Julie McCulloch (Heinemann, 2001)

Websites

www.bbc.co.uk/indianfoodmadeeasy
Information about ingredients, regional cooking and recipes.

www.easy-kids-recipes.com/indian-recipes.html
Indian recipes for main meals and snacks.

www.foodbycountry.com/Germany-to-Japan/India.html
General information about India, and recipes.

www.food-india.com
Recipes, articles, etiquette, guidelines and tips on putting together a menu.

www.indianfoodforever.com
Lots of recipes to try, together with special features about regional food.

Index